LISA GODDARD

ISBN: 978-1-955904-26-1

Cover Photography Copyright © 2022 Linda Pianigiani
Interior Photography by Linda Pianigiani, Gary Gifford, Michaella Page, Lisa Goddard
All rights reserved
Cover and typeset by Matthew Revert

CLASH Books
Troy, NY

Distributed by Consortium

TABLE OF CONTENTS

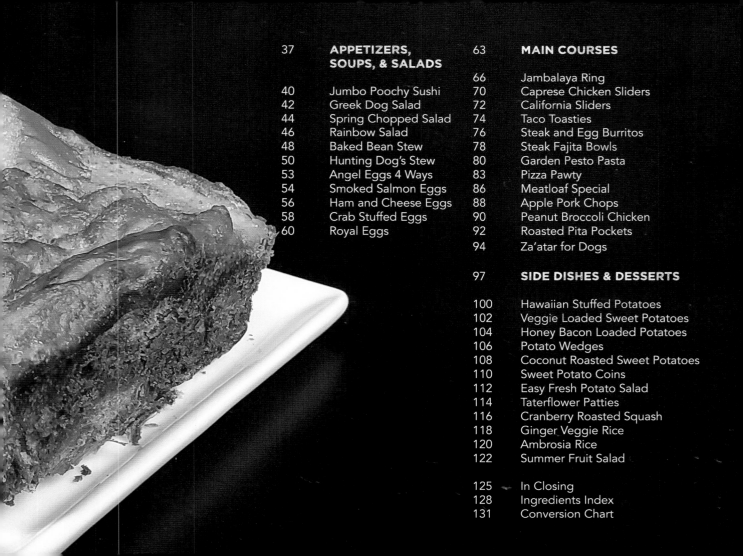

INTRODUCTION

When I think about my life so far, I instinctively view it all through the lens of food. I was raised in New Jersey on home-cooked American classics thanks to my Army veteran father, along with Korean treats thanks to my mother's heritage. My own cooking experience was limited back then, but I did love baking brownies when I had the opportunity. Every once in a while my father would come home from work with a pizza box or Chinese takeout cartons in a brown paper bag, instantly transforming an ordinary weeknight into a party. When I recall my school studies and extracurriculars, I also remember the times heading home from a school event, when my parents would sometimes impulsively turn the car into a diner parking lot for massive portions of made–from–scratch meatloaf, french fries, and so many different kinds of pie like only a diner could offer. Birthdays and other special occasions meant dinner reservations at a cozy local restaurant followed by cake at home. My formative years were fortunately very well–fed ones.

For college I returned to my birthplace, California, where I was able to indulge in the plethora of fresh produce and global cuisine around every corner. This stoked my curiosity so much that I dove into everything food–related any chance I had. I tried flavors I hadn't tried before and consumed all the food news and media I could. I taught myself about California cuisine and fusion and Alice Waters and Wolfgang Puck. My phone calls to my parents back home sometimes veered to food, and I would furiously write down all the tips and recipes they would tell me. I also quickly learned from my cooking mistakes, like when I first made my father's jambalaya recipe, which called for one cup of rice. After adding it, it seemed to disappear into all the liquid, so I decided to add more, not realizing how much the rice would expand, leaving me with some very rice–heavy jambalaya. In Los Angeles I immersed myself in the region's food culture the way a diehard sports fan tracks their favorite team. When not working my office job, I was collecting cookbooks, browsing farmers' markets and grocery stores, and cooking up a storm in my kitchen for myself and for friends, and I haven't stopped since. Basically, food has been, and continues to be, my primary passion.

Across television and social media, I have closely followed great culinary minds like Emeril Lagasse, Nancy Silverton, Carla Hall, Roy Choi, Jose Andres, and so many more I admire. They each have a talent for putting their own spin on an ordinary dish, a spin that shows what is meaningful to them. Whether that's Jamie Oliver demystifying healthy food, making it as easy to make as it is mouthwatering, or Hannah Hart taking the stress out of cooking and encouraging home cooks like me to have fun. They have inspired me and shaped how I think about cooking.

Like others during the pandemic in 2020, I found myself out of an office job, freeing up a lot of my time, much of which I was happy to spend with my dog. I got my dog, a Boston Terrier named Stitch, when he was just ten weeks old, and he is now over fifteen years old. Boston Terriers were originally bred to be human companions, and my dog has indeed gone on quite a few adventures with me over the years. I have always cared for him with gusto, exercising him, socializing him, teaching him obedience, getting him to the vet whenever needed, and feeding him as best as I can. I want him to live as long and as happily as possible. Over the years, I have cooked dog food for him and occasionally given him nutritious "people food," as well as special treats here and there. Finding myself home nearly around–the–clock and cooking a lot more during 2020, in the spirit of pandemic self–care I wanted to share more of my "people food" with him. Since much of what I like to eat contains ingredients that can be dangerous to dogs, such as onions and garlic, I had to carefully make alterations or split recipes into what I would eat versus what he would get. I had become a sort of very specific short-order cook, and the extra effort became tiring. This inspired me to develop single recipes that both he and I could enjoy together. They needed to be delicious enough for me but also completely safe for him.

My first mission was to create a healthy muffin that I could bring along on a hike with my dog or share with him at home as a breakfast snack. It included blueberries, bananas, and peanut butter for their natural sweetness, so there's no need for added sugar in the recipe. I also used oats and an egg for more vitamins, protein and texture. I didn't want to use butter if I didn't have to, so I developed a clean applesauce without added sugar that would function as a butter substitute in the muffins. My dog enjoys raw apple slices, but he absolutely loves the Simple Applesauce. His buggy eyes were open wide in disbelief the entire time he was lapping it up. The final winning muffin recipe was such a big hit with my dog it seemed like he couldn't eat it fast enough. The final product along with my dog's enthusiasm kicked off my quest to develop more recipes that we would both relish.

I cooked for hundreds of hours to develop delicious and dog–friendly recipes, experimenting with different techniques and ingredients until my taste buds were satisfied. During this time, I realized that there were likely other dog parents, and most definitely other dogs, who would want to enjoy these meals too, so I set out to compile the final recipes into this cookbook. Like the chefs I admire so much, I have worked to transform familiar dishes, with my twist of making them dog–friendly, and I hope that this cookbook honors the joy that both food and dogs bring to everyday life.

Delicious Dishes for You and Your Dog is for dog owners who want to spoil their dog with a home–cooked meal, but don't want to cook twice. The spectrum of dishes ranges from quick breakfasts to impressive dinners, designed to be pleasing to both people and puppy palates, as well as non–toxic to dogs. I made things I like to eat as tasty as possible while hacking them so they would be dog–friendly – meatloaf, pizza, sliders, deviled eggs, veggie sushi, and more. I'll walk you through every step needed to create a special meal that you can share with your fluffy sidekick without any guilt.

I want this cookbook to make you the star of the dog park. I want you to be able to serve up something drool–worthy for any dog– (or non–dog) related occasion. I want your social media posts to make you look like the best doggone pup parent ever. Even if you aren't great in the kitchen, as long as you follow the recipes, you'll without fail have at least made dog food that your doggy will love.

This cookbook was made with lots of thought, research and love. I wish everyone happy meals and even happier dogs. They give us so much, I feel like this is the least we can do to return the unconditional love, loyalty and companionship they provide.

Happy cooking, from my kitchen to yours,

Lisa Goddard

PUP TALK

I am so excited for you to discover a new way of cooking – a way to satisfy both you and your dog. I created this array of recipes for you to enjoy making and sharing with your pup, every single one of them safe for dogs to consume.

You benefit too because while designing them to be dog–friendly, they became healthier for humans in the process, by focusing on high–quality nutrient–dense ingredients, increasing antioxidants and anti–inflammatories, and avoiding added salt and sugar.

First, a few important notes about cooking for your dog:

- Before serving any of these dishes, it is recommended to speak with a veterinarian about your dog's diet, especially if the dog has allergies, diabetes, or other health issues or is still a puppy with a developing immune system. While I have self–educated myself on nutrition, health, and safety, I am not a doctor or veterinarian.
- Serving size for dogs should be relative to their body size and their typical daily food consumption. Some dogs have difficulty digesting too–large amounts of even the healthiest foods.
- If your dog shows any sign of distress while eating, contact a veterinarian immediately.
- Let hot dishes cool off before serving to dogs, so they don't burn their mouths.
- The ingredients listed for these recipes are whole foods wherever possible, but some pre–packaged or processed ingredients are occasionally needed. For these ingredients, like bread or sausage, read the nutrition facts labels before purchasing to make sure they do not contain anything poisonous or problematic for dogs such as xylitol, glycerin, onions, garlic, grapes, apple cores, raisins, cinnamon, chocolate, caffeine, or macadamia nuts.

And a few key ingredient notes:

- Since oil and Kosher salt are pantry staples for cooking, they do not appear in the ingredients lists. When a recipe's instructions call for "oil" I recommend using olive oil or avocado oil for the most health benefits, but if needed you may use vegetable oil, canola oil, or peanut oil. If a recipe needs a specific type of oil, like coconut oil, this will be specified in the ingredients list.
- Stocks add flavorful moisture but if you cannot find the stock you need at your store, you can replace it with no/low–sodium broth that is free of garlic or onion. If all else fails, you can even substitute water, although some flavor will be lost in the final dish.
- Certain foods naturally contribute sweetness and saltiness, such as honey and cheese, and I have relied on such ingredients to provide necessary pops of flavor. If you or your dog are on a special diet for health reasons, please keep in mind that a recipe noted as not requiring added salt or sugar may still have, for example, a considerable amount of sodium from bacon. I encourage you to experiment with these recipes as needed to suit your personal goals and guidelines.

Enjoy sharing your love and your meal with your best bud, and I hope this helps you start some new family meal traditions. BONE APPÉTIT!

BREAKFAST
& BRUNCH

BREAKFAST & BRUNCH

Everyone starts their day the same way: by waking up. But before you even open your eyes, there are a number of things that will determine whether or not your morning will be a good one. Is the weather beautiful or dreary? Is there construction happening across the street? Is there anything to eat? Did you get enough sleep? While many dogs are early risers and practically function as alarm clocks for their households, if you and your dog like to sleep in, you are not alone. Slipping out of the comfort of your bed can be a challenge all on its own. What if you hit snooze one more time? Or what if you decide that you would be willing to get up if only you had a nice breakfast to enjoy?

It is often cited that breakfast is the most important meal of the day, and one reason this saying holds true is because your morning can set the tone for the rest of your day. And what is more relevant to your morning than the first thing you eat? I want to share with you my delectable breakfast recipes that will entice you out of slumber and make getting up a little more pleasurable for you and your pupper. Dogs and humans alike will go from snoring to snacking in record time from the first sniff of these morning dishes.

Before writing this book, I was putting in twelve–hour days in an office job. I understand feeling drained and lacking the motivation to get into the kitchen. All I wanted to do was rest. But rest is only part of the rejuvenation equation. Not only must we rest, but we must eat. Plus, if you can avoid eating alone, you can also revitalize your spirits with companionship. I told myself that if I couldn't have a brunch with friends, then I would have one with my dog. This simple act made me realize that taking the time to have a little breakfast in the quiet of the early morning with my fur baby allows me to collect myself and start my day with a positive outlook.

Even if you don't have time to cook in the morning, many of these recipes can be made ahead and frozen or refrigerated for an easily reheated morning meal. I have included recipes from sweet to savory in order to satisfy every morning craving, like my rustic Blueberry Oat Mini Muffins and my rich Sausage and Spinach Frittata. Need a quick breakfast to take on the go? Wrap up a Brunch Sandwich with Orange Honey or whip up my refreshing Tropical Smoothie, with enough for both you and your furry friend. While there is nothing wrong with cereal or puppy chow, a homemade breakfast will give you the feeling of self–indulgence that you and your dog deserve. So go ahead – I give you permission to pamper yourselves with a mouthwatering spread to start your day on the right foot – and the right paw.

BLUEBERRY
OAT MINI
MUFFINS

I like making a batch of these just to have around the house as easy weekday treats and to bring on impromptu hikes with my best friend. I use a mini muffin tin because these muffins are super packed with energy and are best in small portions. This recipe includes notes for those who only have access to a regular–sized muffin tin but know that they can be a bit heavy or dense when full–size.

Makes 36 mini muffins or 12 regular–sized muffins

✓   Vegetarian
✓   No added sugar

INGREDIENTS

⅓ c Simple Applesauce, from recipe at end of this section
1 ½ c mashed bananas (about 3 bananas)
¾ c smooth peanut butter
1 large egg
1 ¼ c old fashioned rolled oats
¾ c all–purpose flour
1 tsp baking soda
1 c blueberries

INSTRUCTIONS

1.   Preheat oven to 350 degrees. Prepare a nonstick muffin tin by spraying the muffin cups with oil or inserting liners.
2.   In a bowl, combine the wet ingredients: Simple Applesauce, bananas, peanut butter, and egg.
3.   In a separate bowl, combine the dry ingredients: oats, flour, baking soda, and ½ tsp Kosher salt.
4.   Stir the dry ingredients into the wet ingredients and continue stirring until combined and a doughy batter begins to form.
5.   Gently fold the blueberries into the batter until evenly distributed. Fill the prepared muffin cups with batter.
6.   Bake in the oven until a toothpick inserted into the center of a muffin comes out clean, about 15 minutes for mini muffins or 25 minutes for regular–sized muffins. Remove from oven and let cool slightly in the pan before removing and serving.

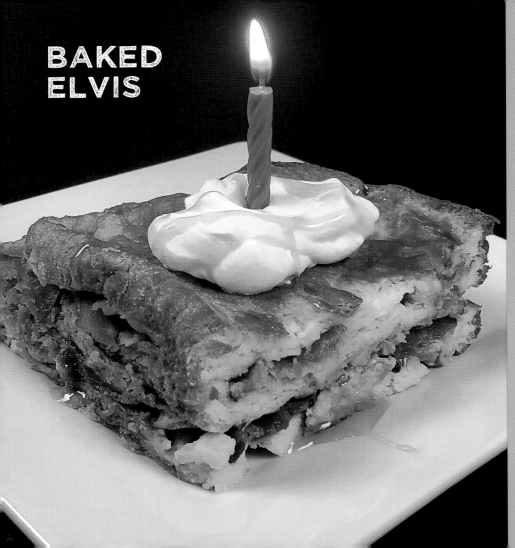

BAKED ELVIS

This mashup of French toast with one of Elvis Presley's rumored favorite sandwiches is like a fluffy sweet eggy three–layer cake. Indulge in it for a special occasion like Father's Day or with candles for a birthday.

Serves 8

✓ Vegetarian–adaptable – simply omit the bacon
✓ No added sugar or added salt

INGREDIENTS

12–16 oz sliced bacon, cut crosswise at one–inch intervals
6 large eggs
1 ½ c unsweetened coconut milk
3 bananas
½ c smooth peanut butter
¾ c Simple Applesauce, from recipe at end of this section
1 lb sliced white bread, about 18 slices
1 c heavy cream
honey, for drizzling

INSTRUCTIONS

1. Preheat oven to 350 degrees.
2. Working in batches, cook the bacon in a nonstick pan over medium–high heat, stirring occasionally, until almost crisp, about 8 minutes. Using a slotted spoon or fork, transfer the bacon to a paper towel lined plate and set aside.
3. In a bowl, whisk the eggs and coconut milk.
4. In a separate bowl, use a fork to mash together the bananas, peanut butter, and ¼ c Simple Applesauce until thoroughly combined.
5. Spread the remaining ½ c Simple Applesauce on the bottom of a 9x13 baking dish.
6. Submerge one bread slice in the egg–milk mixture to coat. Hold the slice up to let excess mixture drip off of it, then place it in the baking dish. Repeat this with additional slices of bread until there is an even single layer of bread in the baking dish; it should take about 6 slices of bread. Spread one–third of the banana mixture over the layer of bread. Scatter half of the bacon over that.
7. Repeat step 6. Then top with a final layer of bread dipped in egg–milk mixture followed by the remaining banana mixture.
8. Cover the baking dish tightly with aluminum foil and bake in the oven for 30 minutes. Uncover and continue baking until a toothpick inserted into the middle of the dish comes out clean, 20–30 more minutes.
9. Beat the heavy cream in a stand mixer, starting at a low speed, increasing to high as it thickens, until the cream is whipped into stiff peaks.
10. Top each serving with whipped cream and drizzle with honey.

SAUSAGE
SPINACH
FRITTATA

Make this savory frittata for a satisfying brunch any day of the year and enjoy the health boost from all the herbs and spices. Any leftovers will keep well and can also be easily repurposed into on–the–go breakfast burritos by just wrapping them in tortillas with avocado slices.

Serves 6

- ✓ Gluten–free
- ✓ Vegetarian–adaptable – simply replace the sausage with a meat substitute
- ✓ No added sugar or added salt

INGREDIENTS

8 oz ground Italian sausage
6 large eggs
¼ c unsweetened coconut milk
1 tbsp chopped fresh parsley
1 tsp dried rosemary
1 tsp dried thyme
½ tsp ground turmeric
1 c loosely packed chopped spinach
½ c shredded cheddar
1 c shredded mozzarella

INSTRUCTIONS

1. Preheat oven to 400 degrees.
2. Add the sausage to a 10– or 12–inch ovenproof nonstick pan over medium–high heat. Cook, stirring and breaking up the sausage, until lightly browned, about 8 minutes. Using a slotted spoon or fork, transfer the sausage to a paper towel lined plate, reserving the sausage drippings in the pan.
3. In a bowl, whisk the eggs, coconut milk, parsley, rosemary, thyme, and turmeric. Fold in the spinach, cheddar, and ½ c mozzarella. Stir in the cooked sausage.
4. Heat the reserved sausage drippings in the pan over medium–high heat. Pour the frittata mixture into the pan, do not stir, and cook undisturbed for 1–2 minutes, until the edges start to set.
5. Transfer the pan to the oven and bake for 15 minutes, until the top is set and just starting to brown. Remove from oven. Sprinkle the remaining ½ c mozzarella on top. Once the heat of the frittata has melted the mozzarella, cut the frittata into wedges and serve.

BRUNCH SANDWICHES WITH ORANGE HONEY

Energize for the day with this meaty, cheesy sandwich, naturally sweetened with a bright citrus honey that will have you and your pup wanting it at every meal. Feel free to skip the English muffin or replace it with a small bagel, dinner roll, sturdy biscuit, or even a large lettuce leaf.

Serves 6

✓ No added sugar or added salt

INGREDIENTS

6 English muffins
3 oz mild cheddar cheese
⅓ c fresh orange juice
¼ c honey
½ tsp ground fennel
1 lb mild or sweet ground sausage
6 eggs

INSTRUCTIONS

1. Preheat oven to 325 degrees. Halve the English muffins and place them cut–side up on a baking sheet. Evenly arrange the cheese across the bottom halves of the muffins. Transfer the baking sheet to the oven to toast the muffins and melt the cheese, about 10 minutes. Turn off the heat and leave in oven to keep warm.
2. In a small saucepan over medium–high heat, whisk together the orange juice and honey and bring it to a boil. Once boiling, reduce heat to low and stir in the fennel. Let simmer for 5 minutes, then turn off the heat.
3. Shape the sausage into 6 patties that are slightly larger in circumference than the English muffins. Cook the sausage patties in a nonstick pan over medium–high heat until cooked through, about 5 minutes per side. Place the cooked sausage patties in a shallow dish or bowl and add the orange honey to coat each patty.
4. Whisk the eggs and then add them to the nonstick pan. Cook the eggs over medium heat, stirring occasionally to scramble, until cooked through, about 3 minutes.
5. To assemble: Arrange the cheese–covered muffin bottoms on a clean work surface. Divide the scrambled egg evenly among the muffin bottoms, then top with sausage patties followed by the muffin tops.

TROPICAL
SMOOTHIE

Smoothies are so versatile – they can be hydrating post–hike treats, healthy desserts, light breakfasts, or happy hour mocktails. For a boozy cocktail, spike the human servings by adding 1 oz of vodka to a 10 oz smoothie.

Serves 4; Makes 40 oz

✓   Gluten–free
✓   Vegetarian
✓   No added sugar or added salt

INGREDIENTS

1 ½ c unsweetened coconut milk
½ c orange juice
10 oz frozen pineapple
10 oz frozen mango
Juice of 1 lime

Lime wedges, optional garnish for humans

INSTRUCTIONS

1. Combine all ingredients except the lime wedges in a blender and blend until smooth.
2. Serve garnished with a lime wedge for humans.

BERRY GOOD SMOOTHIE

You and your pup will love the sweet berries and bananas in this smoothie while benefitting from its protein, antioxidants, and breath–freshening mint. If your dog is an ice cube lover, freeze some blended smoothie in ice cube trays to bust out on a hot day.

Serves 4; Makes 40 oz

✓ Gluten–free
✓ Vegetarian
✓ No added sugar or added salt

INGREDIENTS

1 c plain nonfat Greek yogurt
¾ c unsweetened coconut milk
2 bananas
10 oz frozen strawberries
1 tbsp honey
fresh mint leaves, for garnish

INSTRUCTIONS

1. Combine all ingredients in a blender and blend until smooth.
2. Serve garnished with mint leaves.

SIMPLE APPLESAUCE

Just two ingredients make up this simple side dish or snack that gets all its sweetness from concentrating apples. This applesauce is also a great butter alternative when baking and plays that role in some of the recipes in this book. Avoid using green apples or other tart or sour apples; any other kind of apple will do such as red delicious, fuji, or honeycrisp.

Makes about 3 ½ c applesauce

✓ Gluten–free
✓ Vegetarian
✓ No added sugar or added salt

INGREDIENTS

3 lbs apples

Peel of 1 lemon (leaving behind the bitter white pith)

INSTRUCTIONS

1. Put the lemon peel in a large pot with one inch of water.
2. Peel and core the apples, making sure to discard the entire core, skin, seeds, and any leaves or green parts.
3. Chop the apples into a medium dice. Add them to the pot with the lemon peel and add more water as needed to keep the apples covered by one inch of water. Cover and bring to a boil over high heat. Once boiling, reduce heat to medium and continue cooking until the apples are soft, about 20 minutes.
4. Discard the lemon peel. Drain the apples and return them to the pot. Mash with a potato masher or in a blender until the sauce reaches your desired consistency.
5. Store covered in a refrigerator or freezer.

APPETIZERS,
SOUPS, & SALADS

APPETIZERS, SOUPS, & SALADS

There are certain truths in life, and I believe that one of them is that everyone loves a good appetizer. If you were anything like ten–year–old me at a restaurant, the only section of the menu I ever really needed was the appetizers. Nearly everything was deep fried, crispy brown, and came with fun dipping sauces. When a server would approach with a basket of chicken wings or cheesy bread, I would be standing and applauding them on the inside. I never even knew how hungry I was until the appetizers arrived at the table.

My dog would join me in this lust for appetizers, as I discovered during a particularly eventful dinner party one night. A friend of mine had invited us over, and she had prepared a charcuterie board for the humans to enjoy as an appetizer in her living room before dinner. My dog and hers became acquainted while the humans sipped wine and caught up over tasty bites of fancy cheese and crackers and ribbons of thinly sliced salami and prosciutto. Before we knew it, dinner was ready, so we moved into her dining room. Halfway through dinner we noticed a silence that felt unusual given our dogs' penchant for constant motion and sniffing. We got up and started looking for the dogs, and found them soon enough, lying on a rug under the charcuterie board, and we realized we had left the board unattended and within paw's reach during dinner. Nearly an entire block of cheese had disappeared since dinner began and all context clues pointed to my dog as the culprit.

Since my dog's cheese theft and my early appetizer days of greasy snacks, I now make sure we whet our appetites with healthier but still drool–worthy starters. In this section I share with you our greatest hits, including my Jumbo Poochy Sushi and my Greek Dog Salad. Heartier dishes like my Hunting Dog's Stew signal to the stomach that it is in for warm and filling fare. There is something in this section to complement every dinner plan. I also suggest mixing and matching these recipes together to serve as a meal entirely made of so–called appetizers.

If you and your dog are like me and enjoy attending small dinner parties or potlucks, you may have found yourself stumped trying to think of what to bring. If you are ever unsure, consider contributing one of the soups, salads, or appetizers in this section. They are easy to make in small or large quantities, so you can be a dinner party hero, walking in with a ready–to–eat dish that won't step on the toes of a main course. And what's better than bringing food that, if dropped on the floor, can be immediately gobbled up by a furry four–legged vacuum? These finger foods and small dishes are flavor hits among hounds and humans alike. Show up with one of my recipes, and you will be sure to have a doggone good time and get invited back again and again.

JUMBO
POOCHY
SUSHI

This sushi roll is a delicious and fun way to get more veggies. This can be easily doubled or tripled to make ahead and keep refrigerated for a crowd. Humans may enjoy theirs served with soy sauce or wasabi.

Makes 30 pieces; Serves 5–10

✓ Gluten–free
✓ Vegetarian
✓ No added sugar or added salt

INGREDIENTS

1 c uncooked sushi rice, aka sweet rice aka medium grain rice
1 tbsp + ½ tsp apple cider vinegar
1 tsp fresh lemon juice
1 carrot, peeled and julienned
1 cucumber or ½ English cucumber, peeled and julienned (seeds discarded)
1 avocado, sliced (skin and pit discarded)
5 sheets of unsalted seaweed, aka nori

INSTRUCTIONS

1. Cook the rice per package instructions. Fluff, transfer to a bowl with 1 tbsp apple cider vinegar, and mix. Cover and let cool to room temperature.
2. Combine the remaining ½ tsp apple cider vinegar with the lemon juice. Toss half of this vinegar–lemon mixture with the carrot and cucumber. Gently fold the other half of the vinegar–lemon mixture with the avocado until coated.
3. Arrange the seaweed in a single layer on a work surface. Spread rice on top to cover each sheet of seaweed. Divide the carrot, cucumber, and avocado evenly among each sheet and arrange them in a line across the center of each sheet.
4. Slowly roll up each sheet into a tight cylinder and cut crosswise into 6 even pieces.
5. Serve as–is for dogs. For humans, serve with low–sodium soy sauce and wasabi on the side.

GREEK
DOG
SALAD

Your dog doesn't need to be Greek to enjoy this refreshing salad. Make it an entree by adding some cooked cubed chicken.

Serves 4-6

✓ Gluten–free
✓ Vegetarian
✓ No added sugar or added salt

INGREDIENTS

1 tbsp fresh lemon juice
½ tbsp chopped fresh dill
½ tbsp chopped fresh oregano leaves
1 14.5 oz can chickpeas, rinsed and drained
10 oz cherry or grape tomatoes, halved
2 cucumbers or 1 English cucumber, cut lengthwise into quarters and crosswise at half-inch intervals (seeds discarded)
1 c pitted Kalamata olives, halved, rinsed well to remove any excess salt
¼ c feta crumbles

INSTRUCTIONS

1. In a bowl, whisk the lemon juice, dill, oregano, and 2 tbsp oil.
2. Add the chickpeas, tomatoes, cucumber, and olives. Toss to combine.
3. Top with crumbled feta.

SPRING
CHOPPED
SALAD

This veggie–packed salad tastes like a fresh spring morning, and the greens are chopped small enough so that picky eaters can't eat around them.

Serves 4–6

- ✓ Gluten–free
- ✓ Vegetarian-adaptable - simply omit the chicken
- ✓ No added sugar or added salt

INGREDIENTS

¾ c uncooked quinoa
8 oz boneless skinless chicken breasts, diced
1 zucchini, diced
1 yellow squash, diced
8 oz asparagus, bottoms of stalks removed, chopped crosswise at half–inch intervals
1 c corn kernels
2 tbsp fresh lemon juice
¼ c roughly chopped parsley leaves
1 avocado, cubed (skin and pit discarded)
1 head of Romaine lettuce, chopped
1 tomato, diced (core and seeds discarded)
1 14.5 oz can chickpeas, rinsed and drained

INSTRUCTIONS

1. In a pot, combine the quinoa with 1 ½ c water and bring to a boil over high heat. Once boiling, cover, reduce heat to low, and let simmer until done, 20 minutes. Fluff with a fork and transfer to a bowl.
2. Heat ½ tbsp oil in a nonstick pan over medium–high heat. Add the chicken and cook, stirring occasionally, until cooked through, about 5 minutes. Transfer to the bowl with the quinoa.
3. Cook the zucchini and yellow squash in the remaining drippings in the pan, adding more oil if needed, until starting to brown, about 10 minutes; transfer to the bowl.
4. Combine 1 tsp oil and the asparagus in the pan and cook until browning, 8–10 minutes; transfer to the bowl. Cook the corn in the pan until browning, about 5 minutes; transfer to the bowl.
5. In a small bowl, whisk the lemon juice with 4 tbsp oil until thoroughly combined. Stir in the parsley. Gently fold in the avocado until it is coated.
6. Add the lettuce, tomato, and chickpeas to the bowl with the quinoa, chicken, and vegetables and toss to combine. Gently fold in the dressing and avocado.

RAINBOW
SALAD

This vibrant pasta salad brings together a colorful array of veggies in an easy dressing and is delicious at any temperature although I like it best chilled. Short pasta works best but you can substitute another shape if you prefer. If you want more protein, simply mix in a can of drained and rinsed beans or a chopped cooked chicken breast at the end.

Serves 4–6

- ✓ Gluten–free–adaptable– simply use a gluten– free pasta
- ✓ Vegetarian
- ✓ No added sugar or added salt

INGREDIENTS

1 lb baby carrots, halved crosswise
2 yellow squashes, cut into roughly half–inch pieces
2 c shredded purple cabbage
½ lb short dried pasta such as ditalini, small shells, or orzo
10 oz spinach
¾ c jarred roasted red peppers, rinsed and patted dry
1 ½ tbsp apple cider vinegar
½ tsp dried thyme
½ tsp dried rosemary

INSTRUCTIONS

1. Preheat oven to 400 degrees.
2. Arrange the carrots and squash in an even layer on a rimmed baking sheet lined with parchment paper. Spray or drizzle over about 1 tbsp oil and toss to lightly coat. Transfer to oven to roast for 30 minutes or until carrots can be easily pierced with a fork. Transfer to a large mixing bowl.
3. Heat 1 tsp oil in a medium pot over medium high heat. Add the cabbage and stir to coat the cabbage in the oil. Cook, stirring occasionally, until soft, about 10 minutes. Transfer the cabbage to the bowl with the carrots and squash and return the pot to the stove.
4. Add water to fill two–thirds of the pot and bring to a boil over high heat. Add the pasta and reduce heat to medium. Cook until the pasta is soft, about 8 minutes, stirring in the spinach for the last 2 minutes. Drain the pasta and spinach and transfer to the bowl with the vegetables.
5. Dice the roasted red peppers and add to the bowl.
6. In a small bowl whisk together the apple cider vinegar, thyme, rosemary, and 3 tbsp oil. Fold this dressing into the pasta and vegetables until evenly distributed.

BAKED
BEAN
STEW

Baking this stew in the oven brings together the complex warmth of a cassoulet with hearty vegetable minestrone and includes black-eyed peas for good luck.

Serves 4-6

✓   Vegetarian
✓   No added sugar

INGREDIENTS

8 oz dried black–eyed peas
32 oz unsalted vegetable stock
½ c breadcrumbs, from 2–4 slices white bread
  that have been toasted and then blended into crumbs
1 ½ tbsp dried parsley, divided
½ c chopped celery
8 oz chopped baby carrots
1 zucchini, chopped

1 c green beans, cut crosswise into one–inch pieces
1 ½ c medium diced russet potato
8 oz can tomato sauce
3 tbsp fresh lemon juice
3 tbsp honey
2 tbsp dried oregano
2 tbsp dried basil

INSTRUCTIONS

1. Sort through the black–eyed peas to remove any broken or shriveled beans or debris. Place them in a large bowl with 4 c water and let sit at room temperature overnight. Drain and rinse the beans and add them to a large pot with the vegetable stock over medium–high heat. Once simmering, cover, reduce heat to low, and cook until the beans are getting tender but still have bite, about 40 minutes. Drain, reserving the cooking liquid.
2. Preheat oven to 400 degrees.
3. In a bowl, combine the breadcrumbs, dried parsley, 1 tsp Kosher salt, and 1 tbsp oil.
4. In a separate bowl, combine the remaining ingredients with the beans and 1 tbsp oil. Transfer to a 9x13 baking dish and pour the reserved cooking liquid over it until the top of the liquid is even with the top of the vegetables and beans. Top with two–thirds of the breadcrumb mixture.
5. Bake in the oven for 20 minutes. Lightly press down on the top with the back of a large spoon so the breadcrumbs absorb a little bit of the liquid. If the dish ever starts to dry out, slowly pour more reserved cooking liquid along the inner sides of the baking dish so as not to disturb the crust.
6. Repeat Step 5. Then top with the remaining breadcrumbs and bake for a final 20 minutes.

HUNTING
DOG'S
STEW

There are numerous versions of "hunter's stew," and finally here is a bowl for the hunter's hard-working hunting dogs. This beefy stew will keep everyone happy and warm, no hunting required.

Serves 4–6

✓ Gluten–free
✓ No added sugar or added salt

INGREDIENTS

3 oz bacon (about 3 slices), cut crosswise at half–inch intervals
12 oz boneless top sirloin steak, cubed
8 oz cubed butternut squash flesh
8 oz baby carrots, halved crosswise
1 c frozen peas
3 c unsalted beef stock
1 c orange juice
1 tbsp chopped fresh rosemary
1 tbsp chopped fresh thyme
½ tbsp ground cumin
1 c uncooked white rice

INSTRUCTIONS

1. Cook the bacon in a large pot over medium–high heat, stirring occasionally, until almost crisp, about 8 minutes. Using a slotted spoon or fork, transfer the bacon to a paper towel lined plate and set aside.
2. Add the steak to the pot and stir to coat it in the bacon drippings. Sear the beef on all sides.
3. Add the butternut squash, carrots, peas, beef stock, orange juice, rosemary, thyme, and cumin. Stir to combine, cover, and bring to a rolling boil.
4. Reduce heat to low, stir in the rice, and cover. Let simmer until the rice is done and the vegetables have softened, 20 minutes.
5. Serve the finished stew topped with the cooked bacon.

ANGEL EGGS 4 WAYS

I reworked the classic deviled egg recipe and created not just one but four versions for humans to enjoy with our angelic furry friends. After you've peeled the boiled eggs, you can set aside an eggshell to let dry throughly and then finely crush into a powder that you can keep in the refrigerator and sprinkle on your dog's food for extra protein and calcium.

Each variation yields 24 egg halves

✓ Gluten–free
✓ No added sugar or added salt

SMOKED
SALMON
EGGS

INGREDIENTS

12 large eggs
½ c plain nonfat yogurt
2 tbsp fresh lemon juice
1 tbsp minced capers
1 tsp finely chopped fresh thyme
1 tsp finely chopped fresh dill
½ tsp smoked paprika
2 oz smoked salmon
1 tsp chopped fresh Italian parsley

INSTRUCTIONS

1. Place the eggs in a pot and cover with water by 1 inch. Cover and bring to a boil over high heat. Once boiling, remove from the heat and let sit for 10 minutes. Transfer the eggs to an ice bath, then dry and transfer the eggs to the freezer for 10 minutes. Peel the eggs and halve each lengthwise. Refrigerate the whites and place the yolks in a bowl.
2. To the egg yolks add the yogurt, lemon juice, capers, thyme, dill, and smoked paprika. Finely chop 1 oz of the smoked salmon and add to the bowl. Use a fork to mash the yolks until smooth and combined with the rest of the ingredients in the bowl. Spoon the mixture into the halved egg whites.
3. Slice the remaining salmon into thin strips. Garnish the eggs with the salmon strips and parsley.

HAM AND
CHEESE
EGGS

INGREDIENTS

12 large eggs
½ c plain nonfat yogurt
¼ c chopped cooked ham or deli ham
2 tbsp fresh lemon juice
1 tsp finely chopped fresh rosemary
½ tsp smoked paprika
2 oz cheddar or smoked Gouda cheese, shredded

INSTRUCTIONS

1. Place the eggs in a pot and cover with water by 1 inch. Cover and bring to a boil over high heat. Once boiling, remove from the heat and let sit for 10 minutes. Transfer the eggs to an ice bath, then dry and transfer the eggs to the freezer for 10 minutes. Peel the eggs and halve each lengthwise. Refrigerate the whites and place the yolks in a bowl.
2. To the egg yolks add the yogurt, ham, lemon juice, rosemary, and smoked paprika. Use a fork to mash the yolks until smooth and combined with the rest of the ingredients in the bowl. Spoon the mixture into the halved egg whites.
3. Evenly divide the cheese over the tops of the filled eggs. Use a handheld kitchen torch to melt the cheese. If you do not have a torch, you can alternatively melt the cheese by placing the eggs on a baking sheet under a broiler for 1 minute.

CRAB
STUFFED
EGGS

INGREDIENTS

12 large eggs
½ lb pasteurized lump crab meat
½ c plain nonfat yogurt
1 tbsp minced capers
½ tsp smoked paprika
½ tsp ground ginger
1 tsp chopped fresh Italian parsley

INSTRUCTIONS

1. Place the eggs in a pot and cover with water by 1 inch. Cover and bring to a boil over high heat. Once boiling, remove from the heat and let sit for 10 minutes. Transfer the eggs to an ice bath, then dry and transfer the eggs to the freezer for 10 minutes. Peel the eggs and halve each lengthwise. Refrigerate the whites and place the yolks in a bowl.
2. To the egg yolks add the crab meat, yogurt, capers, smoked paprika, and ginger. Use a fork to mash the yolks until smooth and combined with the rest of the ingredients in the bowl. Spoon the mixture into the halved egg whites.
3. Garnish the eggs by sprinkling the parsley over them.

ROYAL
EGGS

INGREDIENTS

1 6 oz salmon fillet
12 large eggs
½ c plain nonfat yogurt
2 tbsp fresh lemon juice
1 tbsp minced capers
½ tsp finely chopped fresh thyme
½ tsp finely chopped fresh dill
½ tsp smoked paprika
2 oz caviar

INSTRUCTIONS

1. Preheat oven to 400 degrees. Line a rimmed baking sheet with parchment paper.
2. Place the salmon skin side down on the prepared baking sheet and bake in oven until the fish flakes easily with a fork, about 10–15 minutes. Remove the salmon and separate the skin from the flesh by using a butter knife to pry them apart. Use two forks to break up the salmon flesh into small pieces and set aside to let cool. You can either discard the skin or return it to the oven to crisp up into a tasty treat for your dog.
3. Place the eggs in a pot and cover with water by 1 inch. Cover and bring to a boil over high heat. Once boiling, remove from the heat and let sit for 10 minutes. Transfer the eggs to an ice bath, then dry and transfer the eggs to the freezer for 10 minutes. Peel the eggs and halve each lengthwise. Refrigerate the whites and place the yolks in a bowl.
4. To the egg yolks add the yogurt, lemon juice, capers, thyme, dill, smoked paprika, and cooled salmon flesh. Use a fork to mash the yolks until smooth and combined with the rest of the ingredients in the bowl. Spoon the mixture into the halved egg whites.
5. Garnish the eggs with caviar.

MAIN
COURSES

MAIN COURSES

The main event. The star of the show. When a full plate of scrumptious food is sitting in front of you, the eyes go wide, the stomach rumbles in anticipation, your hands get ready to dive in, and... you feel a paw tap your leg. Under the table and drooling is your dog, wanting in, and why not? Dogs are pack animals and here you are enjoying a feast without them. A little something that is not dry kibble would be nice, wouldn't it? You scan your plate trying to find something they can have too. But wait! You realize you cooked something from this cookbook. So, you confidently grab their bowl and serve them their own portion of my Chinese takeout inspired Peanut Broccoli Chicken or classic American comfort fare like my Apple Pork Chops. Tail wagging and intense concentration take over as they revel in their special meal, right beside their favorite human.

Main courses are an opportunity to tuck into a substantial plate that will leave your belly happy and satiated. However, on top of the physical results of a good main course, there are numerous other pleasant effects. It is a chance for a moment of togetherness, a break from the hectic pace of modern daily life. And cooking up a dazzling main course has been my tried–and–true method for anytime I have wanted to win over somebody. A great main course makes for a memorable meal that can lubricate a business deal or lead to a lifelong friendship. It is a starting point where conversation and change can begin. Knowing what a good main course could do, I was determined to make a standout selection of main course recipes to share with you how to add something special to your table – and underneath it.

Using this section you will not only be cooking the best dog cuisine around, but you will also be exhibiting your culinary prowess by making hit signature dishes that will surely be requested again and again. Some of my favorite childhood dishes have been reimagined including my Meatloaf Special made from scratch with a cheesy surprise in the center and my Pizza Pawty recipe where you can get creative with a variety of different toppings. Your family and friends will have a hard time believing that something like my flavorsome and southern–inspired Jambalaya Ring is meant for two different species, but indeed it works for everyone. I have also included my own Za'atar for Dogs spice blend recipe, which works well outside of this cookbook to liven up anything you or your dog are finding a little bland.

The adjustments I have made to classic recipes so they would be safe for dogs to eat have resulted in them becoming even better, healthier, fresher, and more delicious. Cooking these recipes will get everyone's tongues and tails wagging in delightful anticipation.

JAMBALAYA
RING

This adapted jambalaya is comforting on its own out of a bowl, but it's extra special when finished in a pastry ring, a nod to the Gulf Coast's celebratory King Cake ring. Serve with hot sauce for humans.

Serves 6–8

✓ No added sugar or added salt

INGREDIENTS

8 oz ground sweet Italian sausage
1 green bell pepper, small diced (core/ribs/seeds discarded)
1 stalk celery, small diced
1 tsp paprika
½ tsp cumin
½ tsp dried thyme
½ tsp dried oregano

½ tsp ground fennel
1 14.5 oz can no/low–sodium diced tomatoes, rinsed and drained
1 c unsalted chicken stock
½ c uncooked white rice
2 8 oz cans refrigerated crescent rolls
1 large egg

INSTRUCTIONS

1. Cook the sausage in a pot over medium–high heat, frequently stirring to crumble it up, until browned, about 8 minutes.
2. Add the green bell pepper, celery, paprika, cumin, thyme, oregano and fennel. Cook, stirring frequently, until the vegetables are slightly softened, about 8 minutes.
3. Add the tomatoes and stock and stir to combine, scraping the pot to deglaze. Bring to a boil. Once boiling, reduce heat to low, stir in the rice, and cover. Let simmer for 30 minutes.
4. Serve the jambalaya in bowls if desired. If finishing in a pastry ring, proceed to next step.
5. Let the jambalaya cool completely.
6. Preheat oven to 375 degrees. Prepare a rimmed baking sheet with parchment paper. Whisk the egg with 1 tbsp water and set aside.
7. As pictured, on the prepared baking sheet unroll the crescent roll dough and arrange in a ring, slightly overlapping. Spoon the jambalaya into a thick circular ring along the overlapping portion of the dough. Fold the pointed dough ends into the center of the ring, tucking the ends under the ring if needed.
8. Brush all exposed dough with the egg wash. Bake 20 minutes until the dough is golden brown. Remove and let rest for 5 minutes before slicing and serving.

Unroll the crescent roll dough and arrange in a ring, slightly overlapping

Spoon the jambalaya into a thick circular ring along the overlapping portion of the dough

Fold the pointed dough ends
into the center of the ring,
tucking the ends under the ring

CAPRESE
CHICKEN
SLIDERS

Amp up a plain old chicken sandwich with classic Caprese flavors and splurge on fresh basil when in season. You and your pup don't need to be Italian to savor this sandwich. Your pup may not be very interested in the bun, so feel free to skip it and serve this bun–less.

Makes 12 sliders

✓ Gluten–free–adapable – simply go bun–less
✓ No added sugar or added salt

INGREDIENTS

1 ½ lbs boneless skinless chicken breasts
12 slices dry salami
3 oz mozzarella, thinly sliced or shredded
12 slider buns (optional for dogs), toasted
½ c basil leaves
1 small tomato (core and seeds discarded), cut crosswise into 12 slices

INSTRUCTIONS

1. Place the chicken between sheets of plastic wrap and pound with a mallet or your fist to half–inch thickness. Remove the plastic wrap and cut the chicken into 12 pieces roughly equal in size.
2. Place the salami in an even layer in a nonstick pan over medium heat; you may need to do this in batches. Cook, flipping occasionally, until starting to crisp, 3–5 minutes. Transfer to a paper towel lined plate.
3. Heat 1 tsp oil in the pan over medium–high heat. In batches, cook the chicken in a single layer until one side is done, about 5–7 minutes. Flip the chicken over and evenly distribute the mozzarella on top of the now–exposed cooked side of the chicken. Let cook undisturbed until the chicken is cooked through and the mozzarella is melted, about 5–7 more minutes.
4. To assemble: Arrange the slider bun bottoms on a clean work surface. Divide the chicken evenly among the bun bottoms, then top with basil leaves, salami, and tomato. Top with the slider bun tops.

CALIFORNIA
SLIDERS

Few ingredients are more synonymous with California than avocado and kale. They permeate the local cuisine and are packed with nutritional value. Avocados are generally safe for dogs in small amounts as long as they get only the flesh, so be sure that the skin, pit, and any stem or leaves are discarded. Tossing avocado with lime juice helps to keep browning at bay and adds a welcome tart acidity to cut through the creaminess.

Makes 8 sliders

✓ Gluten–free–adapable – simply go bun–less
✓ No added sugar or added salt

INGREDIENTS

1 lb ground beef
3 oz mild cheddar cheese, thinly sliced or shredded
1 avocado, cubed (skin and pit discarded)
2 tbsp fresh lime juice
1 tomato, diced (core and seeds discarded)
1 c shredded Lacinto kale or lettuce
8 slider buns

INSTRUCTIONS

1. Shape the ground beef into 8 patties that are slightly larger in circumference than the slider buns.
2. Heat 1 tbsp oil in a nonstick pan over medium–high heat until hot. Place the beef patties in the pan in an even layer (you may need to do this in batches). Let the patties cook until halfway done, about 4–5 minutes.
3. Flip over the patties. Divide the cheese into eight even amounts and arrange the cheese on top of the eight patties. Cover the pan with a lid or tented piece of foil and let the patties continue to cook for another 4–5 minutes or until they are cooked through and the cheese has melted. Remove the patties from the pan and set aside to rest.
4. Toss the avocado in a small bowl with the lime juice to coat. Add the diced tomato and gently toss just to evenly distribute the tomato.
5. To assemble: Arrange the slider bun bottoms on a clean work surface. Divide the kale evenly among the bun bottoms, then top with beef patties, followed by the avocado/tomato mixture, then finally the slider bun tops.

TACO
TOASTIES

Rice and bean tacos get sealed into half quesadillas like thin panini, toasty on the outside and satisfyingly filling on the inside. Humans may enjoy these with salsa or hot sauce.

Makes 10 toasties

✓ Vegetarian
✓ No added sugar or added salt

INGREDIENTS

¾ c plain nonfat Greek yogurt
1 avocado, flesh only (skin and pit discarded)
3 ½ tbsp fresh lime juice
2 tbsp cumin
2 14.5 oz cans black beans, rinsed and drained
2 ½ c shredded Mexican blend cheese
2 tbsp honey

1 c cooked white rice
3 tsp fresh cilantro leaves, finely chopped
1 ½ tsp fresh oregano leaves, finely chopped
10 8–inch flour tortillas

INSTRUCTIONS

1. Combine the yogurt, avocado, 1 tbsp lime juice, and 1 tbsp cumin in a food processor, blender, or using a fork in a bowl until smooth. Refrigerate until ready to serve.
2. Mash the beans with the remaining lime juice and cumin, the honey, and 2 ½ tbsp oil into a smooth mixture.
3. In a bowl combine the rice, cilantro, and oregano.
4. Preheat oven to 425 degrees.
5. Place a tortilla on a work surface. Evenly spread 3 tbsp of the bean mixture to cover the tortilla, leaving just ¼–inch space around the edge. Top with ¼ c cheese and pat to adhere the cheese to the bean mixture. Sprinkle 1 ½ tbsp rice mixture over just the left half of the tortilla. Fold the right half over to cover the left side and press to seal.
6. Repeat Step 5 until you have assembled 10 toasties.
7. Arrange the toasties in a single layer across two nonstick baking sheets. Spray oil liberally on both sides of each toastie.
8. Bake in oven for 10 minutes, flipping them over halfway.
9. Serve with the yogurt sauce.

These savory protein–packed wraps could hardly be fresher with their from–scratch easy hash brown potatoes and lightly mashed beans instead of processed refried beans. Some dogs won't care about the tortilla wrap, so you have the option to make them burrito bowls by skipping the tortillas and just serving the filling. Humans may enjoy theirs with a favorite salsa or hot sauce.

Makes 8 burritos

- ✓ Gluten-free-adaptable - simply use gluten-free tortillas or omit tortillas entirely
- ✓ No added sugar or added salt

STEAK AND EGG BURRITOS

INGREDIENTS

¼ c fresh lime juice

2 tbsp cumin

1 tbsp ground fennel

1 lb sirloin tip steak, can also use carne asada,
  skirt steak, flank steak, or ribeye steak if desired

1 14.5 oz can black beans, rinsed and drained

8 slices of bacon (about ½ lb)

2 large russet potatoes (about 1 ½ lbs total), shredded,
  rinsed with cold water, and patted dry

8 oz mild cheddar cheese, shredded

8 large eggs

8 large (at least 10–inches across) flour tortillas

1 avocado, sliced (skin and pit discarded)

INSTRUCTIONS

1. In a shallow container or a plastic zip top bag, thoroughly combine the lime juice, cumin, ground fennel, and 1 ½ tbsp oil. Chop the steak into a small dice and add to the lime marinade. Cover or seal and let the steak sit in the marinade for 30 minutes, tossing halfway.
2. In a small bowl, mash the beans with 1 tbsp oil until all beans have been broken and the mixture is still a bit chunky. Set aside.
3. Cook the bacon in a nonstick pan over medium heat until almost crisp, about 8 minutes. Using a slotted spoon or fork, transfer the bacon to a paper towel lined plate and set aside.
4. Pour off all but 1 ½ tbsp of the bacon drippings from the pan. Add the shredded potato and cook, stirring occasionally, over medium–high heat until cooked through and softened, about 8 minutes. Stir in the cheese until melted, about 30 seconds. Remove from the pan and set aside.
5. Add the steak to the pan with all of its marinade. Cook, stirring occasionally, over medium heat for 5 minutes or until the steak is cooked through to your desired doneness. Remove from the pan and set aside.
6. Whisk the eggs and then add them to the pan. Cook the eggs over medium heat, stirring occasionally to scramble, until almost done, about 2–3 minutes. Turn off the heat.
7. To assemble: Divide the beans, bacon, potato–cheese mixture, steak, scrambled eggs, and avocado evenly among the tortillas' centers. Fold in the left and right sides of each tortilla towards the center, then fold up the bottom of each tortilla over the center, and roll up into a burrito.

STEAK FAJITA BOWLS

Serve this healthy fido fiesta as pictured or mix everything together so picky eaters are more likely to eat everything. Humans may enjoy theirs with a favorite salsa or hot sauce.

Serves 4

✓   Gluten–free
✓   Vegetarian–adaptable – simply omit the steak
✓   No added sugar or added salt

INGREDIENTS

2 tsp dried oregano
1 tbsp + 2 tsp cumin
12 oz steak (sirloin tip, skirt, flank, and carne asada work well)
1 ¼ c unsalted beef stock
¾ c uncooked quinoa
¼ c + 2 tsp + 1 tbsp fresh lime juice
2 tbsp finely chopped fresh cilantro

1 tomato, diced (core and seeds discarded)
1 red bell pepper, small diced (core/ribs/seeds discarded)
1 avocado, cubed (skin and pit discarded)
¾ c plain nonfat Greek yogurt
1 head of Romaine lettuce, shredded
1 14.5 oz can black beans, rinsed and drained

INSTRUCTIONS

1. Combine the oregano and 2 tsp cumin. Rub it all over the steak, then refrigerate the steak for 30 minutes.
2. Bring the beef stock, quinoa, and ¼ c lime juice to a boil in a pot over high heat. Once boiling, reduce heat to low, cover, and let simmer for 20 minutes or until the quinoa has absorbed the liquid. Remove from heat and use a fork to fluff the quinoa and mix in the cilantro.
3. Heat 1 tsp oil in a nonstick pan over medium–high heat. Add the steak and cook, flipping only once, until it reaches your desired doneness, about 5–7 minutes for medium. Remove the steak from the pan and let rest for 10 minutes. Slice it into thin strips that are about 2 inches by ½ inch.
4. Cook the tomato and red bell pepper in the nonstick pan over medium–high heat for 1 minute. Add 2 tsp lime juice and continue cooking until the red bell pepper has softened, 3–5 minutes.
5. Toss the avocado in a small bowl with 1 tbsp lime juice to coat. In a separate bowl, thoroughly combine the yogurt with 1 tbsp cumin.
6. Serve by including some of everything in each bowl with a dollop of the cumin yogurt.

GARDEN PESTO PASTA

I love upgrading my vegetables with fresh herbs for even more flavor and nutritional value. For this comforting pasta, you'll first roast vegetables in a fresh herb oil, and then use fresh herbs to make your own pesto sauce. This dish is best served warm but also travels so well that it would be great on a picnic date with your pup.

Serves 4–6

- ✓ Gluten–free–adaptable – simply use a gluten–free pasta
- ✓ Vegetarian
- ✓ No added sugar

INGREDIENTS

3 tbsp minced fresh herbs – rosemary, thyme,
  or oregano or a combination of these
1 lb baby carrots, each sliced crosswise into thirds
2 zucchini, halved lengthwise and medium diced
2 yellow squashes, halved lengthwise and medium diced
2 red bell peppers (core/ribs/seeds discarded),
  each cut into 6 pieces roughly equal in size

1 lb small dried pasta, such as elbows, corkscrews or bowties
1 c packed fresh basil leaves
¼ c packed fresh parsley leaves
¼ c grated parmesan
¼ c almonds
1 tbsp fresh lemon juice

INSTRUCTIONS

1. Preheat oven to 425 degrees. Line two rimmed baking sheets with parchment paper.
2. In a large mixing bowl, combine the minced fresh herbs with 3 tbsp oil and 1 ½ tsp Kosher salt. Add the carrots, zucchini, and yellow squash, and toss to coat the vegetables in the herb oil. Add the red bell peppers and toss until evenly distributed. Arrange the vegetables in a single layer across the two prepared baking sheets. Place in oven for 20 minutes, tossing once halfway. Transfer the carrots, zucchini, and yellow squash back into the large mixing bowl. Chop the bell peppers into a large dice and add them to the mixing bowl.
3. While the vegetables are roasting, bring 6 c water to a boil over medium–high heat. Add the pasta and cook to package instructions, boiling for about 9 minutes. Drain, reserving 1 c of the pasta cooking liquid, and add the pasta to the large mixing bowl with the vegetables. Toss to combine and set aside.
4. Combine the basil, parsley, parmesan, almonds, lemon juice, and 2 tbsp of the pasta cooking liquid in a blender and blend to form a chunky paste. Then, run the blender at a low speed while slowly drizzling in ¼ c oil to create a bright green creamy sauce. If it looks too dry and lumpy, drizzle in more oil and/or pasta cooking water, one tablespoon at a time, until you achieve a light creamy consistency.
5. Add the sauce to the large mixing bowl and toss until thoroughly combined. If desired, you can add more of the pasta cooking water, one tablespoon at a time, to loosen it up to your preference.

PIZZA PAWTY

Get everyone involved for a pizza making party! It's easy as pie with this no–rise dough and no–cook sauce. Make the plain cheese pizza version or add some of the suggested toppings.

Serves 4

✓   Vegetarian–adaptable – simple omit meat toppings

✓   No added sugar or added salt

INGREDIENTS

CHEESE PIZZA

- 1 15 oz can tomato sauce
- ¼ c minced fresh parsley
- 2 ½ tsp dried oregano
- 1 tsp ground fennel
- 2 c all–purpose flour, plus extra for dusting
- 1 c plain nonfat Greek yogurt
- 1 c shredded part–skim low–moisture mozzarella
- 1 ½ tbsp grated or shredded parmesan

TOPPING VARIATIONS

MEAT LOVERS

- 4 oz ground sausage, sauteed until cooked through and browned
- 4 oz ground beef, rolled into 32 small balls each about half–inch in diameter, sauteed in the sausage drippings until cooked through, about 5 minutes
- 3 oz sliced bacon (about 3 slices), chopped and cooked
- ⅔ c shredded cooked chicken breast (sauté in the sausage drippings then shred)
- 12 slices pepperoni

THE WORKS LITE

- 12 slices pepperoni
- ¼ c sliced black olives, drained and rinsed well under running cold water (to remove any extra sodium)
- 1 green bell pepper (core/ribs/seeds discarded), halved crosswise and thinly sliced and sauteed in ½ tsp oil until cooked through, about 5 minutes

STITCH'S SPECIAL

- ½ c chopped Canadian style bacon aka back bacon
- ½ c chopped pineapple

INSTRUCTIONS

1. Preheat oven to 450 degrees. Line a rimmed baking sheet with parchment paper.
2. If using any toppings, make sure any that need to be cooked have been cooked and completely cooled.
3. Make your pizza sauce by mixing in a bowl the tomato sauce, parsley, oregano, fennel, and 2 tsp oil. Set aside.
4. In a separate bowl, use your hands to combine the flour, yogurt, and 3 tbsp oil until a dough forms and does not stick to your fingers. On a floured surface use a floured rolling pin to roll the dough flat into a ¼–inch thick crust that is rectangular in shape to fit the baking sheet. Once it gets close to the final shape, transfer the crust onto the baking sheet and finish shaping it there. Poke the dough all over with a fork. Bake in oven for 10 minutes. Remove.
5. Spread your pizza sauce all over the crust, followed by your toppings, followed by the mozzarella and parmesan.
6. Bake in oven until the cheese has melted and started to turn golden brown, about 10 minutes.

MEATLOAF SPECIAL

If I had a diner like the ones I grew up frequenting in New Jersey, this meatloaf featuring classic Italian–American flavors would be the special on my menu.

Serves 6

✓   No added sugar or salt

INGREDIENTS

⅓ c finely chopped celery
⅓ c shredded carrots
⅓ c minced fresh parsley
1 lb ground beef
8 oz ground mild Italian sausage
½ c old fashioned rolled oats
2 large eggs
1 tsp dried thyme
1 tsp dried rosemary

3 tsp dried basil
3 tsp dried oregano
2 oz mozzarella
1 14.5 oz can no/low–sodium diced tomatoes, rinsed and drained
2 tbsp honey
1 tbsp fresh lemon juice
4 tbsp breadcrumbs, from 1–2 slices white bread
   that have been toasted and then blended into crumbs
2 tbsp grated or finely shredded parmesan

INSTRUCTIONS

1. In a nonstick pan over medium–high heat cook the celery and carrots in 2 tbsp water and 1 tsp oil, stirring frequently, until softening and the water has evaporated, 3–5 minutes. Stir in the parsley and cook for 1 more minute. Transfer to a bowl and let cool. To the bowl, add the beef, sausage, oats, eggs, thyme, rosemary, 2 tsp dried basil, and 2 tsp dried oregano and combine thoroughly with your hands.
2. Preheat oven to 350 degrees. Place half of the meatloaf mixture in the center of a shallow baking dish and form into an 8–inch by 4–inch rectangle/oval. Press down along the center to create a well and arrange the mozzarella in the well. Place the remaining meatloaf mixture on top of the mozzarella and seal the meat around the edges, keeping the 8–inch by 4–inch shape. Bake in oven for 50 minutes.
3. Mash together the tomatoes, honey, lemon juice, ½ tsp dried basil, and ½ tsp dried oregano and set aside. In a separate bowl, combine the breadcrumbs, parmesan, ½ tsp dried basil, and ½ tsp dried oregano in a small bowl.
4. Use a spatula to add the tomato mixture to the top and sides of the meatloaf, pressing to adhere. Follow with the breadcrumb mixture, pressing it to the top and sides. Return the meatloaf to the oven for 25 minutes. Remove and let rest for 10 minutes before slicing and serving.

APPLE PORK
CHOPS

Take the classic combination of apples and pork to new heights with honey, herbs, and an indulgent bacon accent. Comforting, satisfying, and elevated, this will more than impress and delight both human and dog palates.

Serves 4

- ✓ Gluten–free
- ✓ No added sugar

INGREDIENTS

2 tbsp honey
2 tbsp apple cider vinegar
1 tsp dried thyme
1 tsp dried ground sage
1 tsp dried ground fennel
1 tsp celery seeds
1 lb boneless pork loin chops
1 lb sliced bacon
2 large apples

INSTRUCTIONS

1. Make a marinade for the pork by whisking together the first 6 ingredients (through the celery seeds) with ¼ c oil and ½ tsp Kosher salt. Pat the pork dry with paper towels and place the pork in a zip top bag. Pour the marinade over the pork and seal the bag. Toss the bag to distribute the marinade evenly over all sides of the pork. Place in the refrigerator for 1 hour.
2. Preheat oven to 400 degrees. Evenly coat the bottom of a 9x9 baking dish with ½ tsp oil.
3. Transfer the pork to a work surface, reserving any leftover marinade. Wrap each piece of pork chop in an even layer of bacon slices.
4. Peel and core the apples, making sure to discard the entire core, skin, seeds, and any leaves or green parts. Slice vertically into wedges roughly ¼–inch thick.
5. Arrange the apple wedges to cover the bottom of the baking dish. Arrange the bacon wrapped pork in an even layer on top of the apples. Pour the reserved marinade over the pork.
6. Place the baking dish in the oven for 30 minutes. Remove, flip the pork chops over to their other side, and bake for another 30 minutes. Remove and serve the pork with the cooked apples.

PEANUT
BROCCOLI
CHICKEN

Share this Chinese takeout inspired meal with your pup and any year can be the year of the dog.

Serves 6

✓ Gluten–free
✓ No added sugar or added salt

INGREDIENTS

2 heads broccoli, cut into small florets, cores discarded
⅓ c honey
3 c orange juice
2 tbsp peanut butter
1 tbsp minced fresh ginger
1 tsp sesame oil
1 lb boneless skinless chicken breast or thigh, diced
4 c cooked white rice
1 tbsp sesame seeds

INSTRUCTIONS

1. Preheat oven to 375 degrees.
2. Line a baking sheet with parchment paper and arrange the broccoli on it in a single layer. Place in oven for 30 minutes until roasted and browning. Transfer to a bowl.
3. Whisk the honey into 2 ½ c orange juice in a small saucepan over medium–high heat and bring to a boil. Continue boiling, stirring occasionally, until the mixture has reduced to 1 c. This can take up to 1 hour. Keep a close eye on it and lower the heat if it is in danger of boiling over at any point. Once reduced, vigorously whisk in the peanut butter and ginger until thoroughly combined and warmed through, about 1–2 minutes. Set aside.
4. Heat the sesame oil in a nonstick pan over medium heat. Add the chicken and remaining orange juice and cook, stirring occasionally, until chicken is cooked through, 6–8 minutes. Transfer the chicken to the bowl with the broccoli. Add the honey mixture to the bowl and toss to coat all the broccoli and chicken.
5. Serve the broccoli and chicken over rice, garnished with sesame seeds.

ROASTED
PITA
POCKETS

This Mediterranean rainbow of roasted vegetables with a tzatziki–inspired yogurt sauce makes for comforting customizable pita wraps that are great for a crowd.

Serves 6

✓ Vegetarian
✓ No added sugar

INGREDIENTS

1 ½ tsp Za'atar for Dogs, from recipe at end of this section
½ tsp turmeric
1 ½ lb sweet potatoes, cut into half–inch thick slices
1 lb beets, cut into half–inch thick pieces
1 lb baby carrots, halved lengthwise
1 English cucumber, peeled
1 ½ c plain nonfat Greek yogurt
2 tsp fresh dill, finely chopped
2 tsp fresh lemon juice
6 small pita bread rounds
¼ c jarred roasted red peppers, rinsed and patted dry
¼ c feta crumbles

INSTRUCTIONS

1. Preheat oven to 400 degrees. Line two rimmed baking sheets with parchment paper.
2. In a bowl, whisk the Za'atar for Dogs, turmeric, and 2 tbsp oil. Toss with the sweet potatoes, beets, and baby carrots and arrange in a single layer across the two prepared baking sheets. Place them in the oven until easily pierced with a fork, about 40 minutes.
3. Using the large holes of a box grater, shred the cucumber over a clean kitchen towel. Pat the shredded cucumber dry as well as you can and transfer to a bowl. Add the yogurt, dill, and lemon juice, and combine thoroughly. Set aside; keep refrigerated.
4. Present everything family–style for everyone to design their own pita. Or assemble all of them by evenly dividing the sweet potatoes, beets, and baby carrots among each of the pita bread rounds, topped with yogurt sauce, roasted red peppers, and feta. If you have green leaves from the beets, those may also be added to the pita wraps.

ZA'ATAR FOR DOGS

Za'atar is a warm, nutty, and slightly herby spice mixture, but traditionally it includes marjoram which is toxic to dogs. This is a dog-friendly version of za'atar that happens to also be my favorite za'atar. I always have a batch handy because it adds so much unique flavor to salads, sandwiches, pizza, pasta, and dips, and it has a gorgeous reddish-brown hue.

Makes ½ c

✓ Gluten-free
✓ Vegetarian
✓ No added sugar

INGREDIENTS

1 tbsp whole coriander seeds
1 tbsp whole sesame seeds
1 tbsp sumac
1 tbsp dried thyme
1 tbsp dried oregano
½ tbsp ground cumin
½ tbsp paprika
1 tsp dried rosemary

INSTRUCTIONS

1. Place the coriander seeds in a small nonstick pan over medium heat. Stir frequently until lightly browning, about 3–5 minutes. Transfer the seeds to a mortar and pestle.
2. Place the sesame seeds in the pan and toast, stirring frequently, until slightly browned and the oils start to release, 2–3 minutes. Transfer the seeds to the mortar and pestle.
3. Add the remaining ingredients and ½ tsp Kosher salt to the mortar and pestle and stir to thoroughly combine, crushing the coriander and sesame seeds.
4. The resulting za'atar spice mixture can be stored in an airtight container.

SIDE DISHES
& DESSERTS

SIDE DISHES & DESSERTS

A scrumptious side dish will make quick friends of any human or furry doggo. When it came to developing dog-friendly side dishes and desserts, I focused on featuring healthy vegetables and fruits whenever possible. For me personally, the potato reigns supreme since it is one of my favorite foods. Potatoes are filling, gluten-free, and loaded with nutrients, and they are easy to work with, to dress up, and to store. I eat a lot of potatoes in a variety of ways including baked, fried, and in hash brown form, and I would not be a very happy person if I had to live without potatoes. Potatoes, especially sweet potatoes, are also beneficial for canine digestive systems. In developing the recipes in this section, I made sure to include dog-friendly versions of my favorite potato sides and also found ways to incorporate more nutritious vegetables like cauliflower and squash. Prepare to be pawed at if you give in to making my sweet and savory Honey Bacon Loaded Potatoes or my cheesy and smoky Taterflower Patties. These recipes not only turn out impressive supplemental dishes for your main courses, but can also serve as stand-alone snacks when you get one of those hunger pangs in the middle of the afternoon. Some of the sweeter recipes in this section, like the Sweet Potato Coins, can also function as handy treats or even as dessert.

The word dessert originates from the French verb meaning "to clear the table." It signifies the end of a meal by providing a taste of something different to wash down the big meal that preceded it. As important as dessert is to some people, I must admit I have never had much of a sweet tooth. When I was growing up, dessert was not a standard part of a meal in my family. Unless it was a special occasion, if something sweet was needed, that need would be fulfilled by a piece of fruit like an orange or a small bowl of strawberries. These days, desserts and dessert cafes are everywhere, and there is no requirement to finish a big meal before treating yourself to a little something sweet. I have been known to indulge in a cupcake or freshly baked cookie every now and then, but on the occasions when I feel I need something sweet, my first instinct is to turn to the simplicity of fresh fruit.

Even late at night when I'm watching television on the couch next to my dog, and I want something to snack on, I'll cut up an apple for both of us to share. As it turns out, this fruit–centric dessert palate is ideal for a cookbook in which all the recipes are safe for dogs. I was able to incorporate the fresh fruit I love in the creation of my desserts – my colorful Summer Fruit Salad and my creamy Ambrosia Rice. On top of being shareable with your pooch, they are also gluten–free, vegetarian, packed with disease–fighting antioxidants, and contain no added sugar or salt. At the end of the day, I want you to feel good about what you are putting into you and your dog's bodies, and my dessert recipes will give you the sweetness you crave without using any processed white sugar. Sleeping dogs won't be lying around for long when you cook up any of my tasty side dishes or desserts.

HAWAIIAN
STUFFED
POTATOES

The Hawaiian pizza gets reimagined as a sweet potato beefed up with fresh pineapple, meaty Canadian bacon, melty mozzarella, and a tangy yogurt sauce. Sweet potatoes are excellent for dogs and humans alike, packed with vitamins, fiber, and disease–fighting antioxidants, and renowned for supporting healthy digestion and vision.

Serves 6

✓ Gluten–free
✓ No added sugar or added salt

INGREDIENTS

1 ½ c plain nonfat Greek yogurt
⅓ c fresh lemon juice
1 tbsp chopped fresh dill
2 tsp chopped fresh rosemary
6 oz Canadian bacon slices
6 sweet potatoes
1 ½ c shredded low–moisture part–skim mozzarella
1 pineapple, flesh cut into a medium dice (skin, top, bottom, and core discarded)

INSTRUCTIONS

1. Preheat oven to 450 degrees. Line a rimmed baking sheet with parchment paper.
2. Combine the yogurt, lemon juice, dill, and rosemary in a small bowl and keep refrigerated.
3. Arrange the Canadian bacon on the prepared baking sheet in an even layer. Bake in the oven for 10 minutes, flipping over halfway. Chop each slice into about 8 pieces and set aside.
4. Use a fork to stab each potato on all sides, about 4 pokes per potato. Place the potatoes on the baking sheet and bake in oven until a fork can easily pierce through to the center of each potato, about 45–50 minutes depending on the size of the potatoes.
5. Keeping the potatoes on the baking sheet, slice each potato lengthwise halfway through and fluff the insides with a fork. Add ¼ c mozzarella into each potato. Return to oven for 1–2 minutes, until the mozzarella has melted.
6. To serve, divide the Canadian bacon, diced pineapple, and yogurt mixture evenly among the potatoes.

These vegan loaded potatoes explode with nutrient–dense beans and vegetables, making them hearty enough to be a main course by themselves. Turmeric is an anti–inflammatory powerhouse and gives the yogurt sauce a golden hue, while cumin adds an earthy warmth that complements the beans and cilantro.

Serves 6

✓ Gluten–free
✓ Vegetarian
✓ No added sugar or added salt

VEGGIE LOADED SWEET POTATOES

INGREDIENTS

1 ½ c plain nonfat Greek yogurt
⅓ c fresh lemon juice
1 tbsp cumin
1 tbsp turmeric
6 sweet potatoes
2 c broccoli florets, discard any large pieces of stems

1 zucchini, quartered lengthwise and
  cut crosswise into ¼–inch slices
2 14.5 oz cans black beans, rinsed and drained
¼ c chopped cilantro (optional)
3 c spinach leaves, chopped
⅓ c red bell pepper, small diced (core/ribs/seeds discarded)

INSTRUCTIONS

1. Preheat oven to 450 degrees. Line a rimmed baking sheet with parchment paper.
2. Combine the yogurt, lemon juice, cumin, and turmeric in a small bowl and keep refrigerated.
3. Use a fork to stab each potato on all sides, about 4 pokes per potato. Place the potatoes on the baking sheet and bake in oven until a fork can easily pierce through to the center of each potato, about 45–50 minutes depending on the size of the potatoes.
4. While the potatoes are baking, bring a large pot of water to a boil. Add the broccoli and cook until bright green, about 2 minutes. Drain and transfer the broccoli to a large mixing bowl.
5. Heat ½ tbsp oil in a nonstick pan over medium–high heat. Add the zucchini and cook, stirring occasionally until done and slightly browned, about 8 minutes. Transfer the zucchini to the mixing bowl with the broccoli. To the bowl, add the black beans, cilantro if using, and spinach, and gently mix until combined.
6. Heat 1 tsp oil in the nonstick pan over medium–high heat. Add the red bell pepper and cook until just starting to soften, about 5 minutes. Turn off the heat.
7. To serve, slice each potato lengthwise halfway through and fluff the insides with a fork. Divide the vegetable mixture evenly among the potatoes. Top with dollops of the yogurt mixture. Sprinkle with red bell pepper and serve immediately.

**HONEY BACON
LOADED
POTATOES**

I have consistently relied on some variation of this recipe to keep me alive for years, ever since my college days at Berkeley where I frequented a popular food truck that was dedicated solely to baked potatoes. This elevated recipe includes honey–kissed bacon (a tasty treat by itself) and herby lemon yogurt to cut through the richness of the cheese and bacon.

Serves 6

✓ Gluten–free
✓ No added sugar or added salt

INGREDIENTS

1 ½ c plain nonfat Greek yogurt
⅓ c fresh lemon juice
2 tsp + ¾ tsp chopped fresh rosemary
1 tbsp + 1 tsp chopped fresh thyme
6 russet potatoes
1 lb sliced bacon
⅓ c honey
1 ½ c shredded cheddar cheese

INSTRUCTIONS

1. Preheat oven to 450 degrees. Line a rimmed baking sheet with parchment paper.
2. Combine the yogurt, lemon juice, 2 tsp rosemary, and 1 tbsp thyme in a small bowl and keep refrigerated.
3. Use a fork to stab each potato on all sides, about 4 pokes per potato. Place the potatoes on the baking sheet and bake in oven until a fork can easily pierce through to the center of each potato, about 45–50 minutes depending on the size of the potatoes. Transfer the potatoes to a clean work surface.
4. Place a wire rack over the baking sheet and arrange the bacon on the rack in an even layer. Brush honey on the top side of each bacon slice. Bake the bacon in oven until cooked through, 8–10 minutes. Transfer the bacon, honey side up, onto a paper towel lined plate. Remove the rack from the baking sheet and discard the parchment paper and any bacon fat.
5. Slice each potato lengthwise halfway through and fluff the insides with a fork. Divide the cheese evenly among the exposed centers of the potatoes. Transfer the potatoes to the baking sheet and place in oven until the cheese is melted, 1–2 minutes.
6. To serve, divide the bacon evenly among the potatoes, breaking up the slices as needed. Top with dollops of the yogurt mixture followed by a sprinkling of the remaining thyme and rosemary.

POTATO WEDGES

These potato wedges are better–for–you French fries with a touch of delightful herb salt. Preparing the potato wedges by soaking and rinsing them in cold water followed by really thoroughly drying them removes excess starch and is the key to getting perfectly crispy on the outside and creamy on the inside wedges. These are delicious on their own, but some humans may also enjoy these served with ketchup, ranch or another dipping sauce.

Serves 4–6

✓ Gluten–free
✓ Vegetarian
✓ No added sugar

INGREDIENTS

1 tbsp chopped fresh rosemary
1 ½ lbs russet potatoes

INSTRUCTIONS

1. Preheat oven to 425 degrees. Line a rimmed baking sheet with aluminum foil and place a wire rack on top.
2. Combine the rosemary with 1 tsp Kosher salt in a small bowl, and mash them together with the back of a spoon until well integrated.
3. Cut the potatoes lengthwise into half–inch wedges, placing each wedge in a bowl of cold water immediately after it's cut. Add water to the bowl if needed to keep the potato wedges completely submerged until all the wedges have been cut.
4. Drain the wedges in a colander and rinse them under running cold water. Place them back into a bowl and add fresh cold water to cover. Let sit for at least 5 minutes. Repeat this step 1–2 more times, or until the fresh cold water in the bowl no longer becomes cloudy from the wedges. Drain and dry out the bowl.
5. Transfer the wedges to a clean kitchen towel and dry them very thoroughly on all sides.
6. Place the wedges in the dried bowl and lightly spray them with oil, tossing them as needed to cover all sides with some oil. Sprinkle the rosemary salt over the wedges, tossing to evenly distribute.
7. Arrange the wedges on the prepared wire rack in a single layer and bake in oven until the wedges are browned on the edges and easily pierced with a fork, about 20–30 minutes.

COCONUT
ROASTED
SWEET
POTATOES

This healthy side tastes like an indulgence thanks to hints of sweetness from coconut and sweet potatoes and warm spice notes from cumin and ginger. This has become fondly known in my home as Coco–Ro–Spo for short, and I hope it brings your family the same delicious comfort.

Serves 6

✓ Gluten–free
✓ Vegetarian
✓ No added sugar or added salt

INGREDIENTS

2 lbs sweet potatoes, peeled and cut into a large dice
¼ c coconut oil
¾ tsp ground cumin
¼ tsp ground ginger
¼ c fresh cilantro leaves (optional, for garnish)

INSTRUCTIONS

1. Preheat oven to 425 degrees. Line a rimmed baking sheet with parchment paper.
2. If the coconut oil is more solid than liquid, heat it gently in a saucepan or microwave until it is all liquid. Whisk in the cumin and ginger. Toss with the sweet potatoes to coat.
3. Arrange the sweet potatoes on the prepared baking sheet in a single layer, not touching. Place in the oven and toss every 10 minutes, until the sweet potatoes can be easily pierced to the center with a fork, about 30 minutes total. Do not overcook; do not let the potato pieces get mushy or fall apart when poked.
4. Toss the cooked potato with any remaining coconut oil mixture. Serve garnished with fresh cilantro if desired.

SWEET
POTATO
COINS

This is one of my simplest recipes and happens to also be easy, tasty, and healthy. Many pups battle digestive issues, which this dish can help remedy, as it features the superfood sweet potato accented by antioxidant–rich honey. I like to make a batch of these to keep in the refrigerator for up to 5 days, so I have some handy to "pay" my pup for good behavior with one of these coins.

Serves 4–6

✓ Gluten–free
✓ Vegetarian
✓ No added sugar or added salt

INGREDIENTS

⅓ c honey
1 tsp chopped fresh rosemary
1 tsp chopped fresh thyme
1 ½ lbs sweet potatoes

INSTRUCTIONS

1. Preheat oven to 425 degrees. Line a rimmed baking sheet with aluminum foil and place a wire rack on top.
2. Combine the honey, rosemary, thyme, and ⅓ c oil in a large bowl.
3. Cut the sweet potatoes into "coins" by slicing them crosswise at half–inch intervals. Add the coins to the bowl and toss to completely coat each potato coin in the honey mixture.
4. Arrange the potato coins in a single layer on the prepared rack and place in the oven. After 20 minutes, flip the coins over and return them to the oven until easily pierced with a fork, about 15 more minutes.

EASY
FRESH
POTATO
SALAD

Fresh dill can often be substituted or omitted from recipes without greatly impacting the final dish. For potato salad though, fresh dill is a must, so make this during the warmer months, when fresh dill is in season and easier to get.

Serves 6–8

✓ Gluten–free
✓ No added sugar or added salt

INGREDIENTS

6 oz bacon (about 6 slices), thinly sliced crosswise
3 lbs potatoes, cut into bite–size chunks (russet, red, new, Yukon gold, or fingerling potatoes work well)
1 stalk celery, halved lengthwise, thinly sliced crosswise
1 c plain low–fat yogurt
2 tbsp fresh lemon juice
2 tbsp chopped fresh dill
½ tsp paprika

INSTRUCTIONS

1. Place the bacon in a large pot over high heat and cook until crisp, stirring occasionally, about 10 minutes. Use a fork or slotted spoon to transfer the crispy bacon bits to a paper towel lined plate.
2. Add the potatoes to the pot and toss in the bacon drippings a couple times. Add water to cover the potatoes by an inch. Cover and bring to a boil over high heat. Once boiling, reduce heat to medium and continue cooking until the potatoes are still firm but can be easily pierced with a fork, about 10 minutes. Do not overcook; do not let the potato pieces get mushy or fall apart when poked. Drain and let cool.
3. In a bowl, thoroughly combine the remaining ingredients. Add the roasted potatoes and crumbled bacon and toss to combine.

TATERFLOWER PATTIES

These potato pancakes get a flavor boost from cheddar and a nutritional boost from cauliflower. Make an extra batch to freeze between parchment paper.

Serves 4–6; Makes about 10 patties

✓ Gluten–free
✓ Vegetarian
✓ No added sugar or added salt

INGREDIENTS

1 head cauliflower, cut into florets, core discarded
1 large russet potato
1 large egg, whisked
½ c mild cheddar, shredded
1 tbsp cornstarch
1 tbsp smoked paprika
plain nonfat Greek yogurt, for serving
Simple Applesauce, for serving, from recipe in first section

INSTRUCTIONS

1. Place the cauliflower in a pot with enough water to cover. Cover the pot and bring to a boil over high heat. Once boiling, reduce heat to medium and continue cooking until the cauliflower is soft, about 30 minutes. Drain the cauliflower thoroughly and return to the pot. Mash with a potato masher until smooth.
2. Preheat oven to 425 degrees. Line a baking sheet with parchment paper.
3. Grate the potato over the large holes of a grater into a fine mesh colander. Rinse well under running cold water, then dry thoroughly between two clean kitchen towels.
4. To the pot with the mashed cauliflower, add the potato, egg, cheddar, cornstarch, and smoked paprika, and stir until thoroughly combined.
5. Place ¼ c of the mixture at a time onto the prepared baking sheet and flatten into a ¼–inch thin patty. Repeat, making sure there is at least a sliver of space between each patty, until all the batter is used.
6. Bake in the oven for 30 minutes.
7. Serve with yogurt and Simple Applesauce.

CRANBERRY
ROASTED
SQUASH

I like the deep green and orange colors of acorn squash, but this recipe works for just about any winter squash or small cooking pumpkin. It feels especially festive around the winter holidays.

Serves 4

✓ Gluten–free
✓ Vegetarian
✓ No added sugar or added salt

INGREDIENTS

½ c dried unsweetened cranberries
¼ c fresh lemon juice
3 tbsp honey
2 tbsp butter
2 tbsp coconut oil
½ tsp dried rosemary
½ tsp dried sage
½ tsp dried thyme
1 ½ lb acorn squash, seeded, cut into one–inch–thick wedges

INSTRUCTIONS

1. Preheat oven to 400 degrees.
2. Place a small saucepan over low heat and add all the ingredients except for the squash. Whisk until butter has melted, about 2 minutes. Transfer to a 9x13 baking dish. Add the squash and toss until the squash is coated in the mixture. Arrange the squash in a single layer with a cut side down.
3. Cover the baking dish tightly with aluminum foil and bake in the oven for 20 minutes. Discard the foil and turn the squash to another cut side. Return to oven and let it continue roasting, uncovered, until the thickest flesh of squash can be easily pierced with a fork, about 20–30 minutes.
4. Remove the skin from the squash before serving to dogs. Serve the squash with the remaining sauce and cranberries from the baking dish.

GINGER
VEGGIE
RICE

This lightened–up take on fried rice is best using day–old white rice that has had a chance to dry out in the refrigerator. If you are making the rice day–of, it helps to spread out the cooked rice on a baking sheet and refrigerate it for at least 30 minutes to dry.

Serves 4

✓ Gluten–free
✓ No added sugar or added salt

INGREDIENTS

1 tbsp butter
2 tsp sesame oil
4 large eggs, whisked
1 c carrots, cut into a small dice
1 c frozen sweet peas
2 tsp minced fresh ginger
3 c cooked white rice
1 tsp fish sauce
2 tsp sesame seeds

INSTRUCTIONS

1. In a nonstick pan over medium–high heat, melt ½ tbsp butter with ½ tsp sesame oil.
2. Add the eggs to the pan and cook, stirring occasionally, until cooked through, about 3 minutes. Transfer the eggs to a cutting board, chop, and set aside.
3. Repeat Step 1, then add the carrots and cook, stirring occasionally, until the carrots are cooked through but still firm, about 5 minutes. Stir in the peas and ginger and cook until heated through, about 2 minutes.
4. Add the remaining 1 tsp sesame oil, the rice, and the fish sauce, and stir to combine thoroughly. Once combined, cook for 6 minutes, stirring only once so the rice can sit and get a bit toasted.
5. Remove from heat and lightly fold in the eggs and sesame seeds.

AMBROSIA
RICE

Ambrosia meets rice pudding for extra flavor and creaminess in this refreshing sweet treat. Dogs can eat marshmallows, but since they are so high in sugar, they are best limited to humans only.

Serves 8

✓   Gluten–free
✓   Vegetarian
✓   No added sugar or added salt

INGREDIENTS

1 orange, halved crosswise and segmented
1 pineapple, cut into a medium dice (skin, top, bottom, and core discarded)
1 c uncooked white rice
2 c unsweetened coconut milk
1 tsp honey
1 c strawberries, tops removed, quartered
1 banana, cut in half lengthwise and sliced crosswise
4 tsp chopped almonds
4 tsp shredded unsweetened coconut
½ c mini marshmallows (optional topping, for humans only)

INSTRUCTIONS

1. Place the orange and pineapple in a colander to let excess juices drain.
2. Bring the rice and coconut milk to a light simmer in a saucepan over medium–high heat. Cover, reduce heat to low, and continue simmering for 30 minutes, stirring every 10 minutes. Remove from heat and mix in honey. Refrigerate until cold. Once cold, fluff the rice with a fork.
3. Place all ingredients in a large bowl and toss to combine. Top human portions with a few mini marshmallows, if using.

SUMMER FRUIT SALAD

As a child, my dessert was typically a piece of fruit, so for this I've brought together some of my favorites for an eye–pleasingly colorful salad packed with natural sweetness and an array of vitamins and antioxidants. For a fun presentation, serve the finished fruit salad in the emptied melon halves.

Serves 12

✓ Gluten–free
✓ Vegetarian
✓ No added sugar or added salt

INGREDIENTS

¼ c honey
1 tbsp fresh lemon juice
5 fresh mint leaves
1 cantaloupe, halved
1 personal seedless watermelon, halved
2 c blueberries
2 c blackberries
2 c quartered strawberries, tops discarded
1 tbsp thinly sliced fresh mint
⅓ c shredded unsweetened coconut
½ kiwi, thinly sliced (optional)

INSTRUCTIONS

1. In a small saucepan over medium–high heat, whisk together the honey, lemon juice, and 1 tbsp of water. Add the fresh mint leaves. Continue cooking, stirring frequently until heated through and thoroughly combined into a thin syrup, about 3 minutes. Pour the mixture into a container and chill until cold.
2. Scrape out the inner pulp of the cantaloupe and discard it. Press a small melon baller into the melon flesh until the ball part is completely in the flesh. Then turn the baller clockwise to carve a spherical shape, and pull out the resulting ball that you carved. Place the melon ball into a large bowl and repeat this technique until all the cantaloupe and watermelon flesh has been scooped. Discard any seeds you may come across while working with the cantaloupe and watermelon.
3. To the bowl of melon balls, add the blueberries, blackberries, strawberries, and thinly sliced mint. Pour the chilled honey mixture over the fruit and gently toss to combine. Serve garnished with coconut and kiwi.

IN CLOSING

When I think about all the things that led me to write this book I think about growing up in New Jersey, the diners my father indulged me in, the Korean cuisine my mother introduced me to, and spending summers chasing down the ice cream truck with my brother. I think about how my food world expanded when I moved to California. I get flashes of dinner parties and kitchen experiments gone awry. I recall the cookware and appliances I ruined in my young adulting days and the personal triumphs like finally successfully executing a Thanksgiving dinner for six.

Perhaps the most vital point in my journey came in October of 2006, when I got my dog, Stitch, a happy yet anxious Boston Terrier with a cute grumpy face, a gassy little body, and unusually long legs. My boundless unconditional love for him drove me to figure out ways to spend quality time with him and how to best take care of him. He has a car seat, a stroller, a variety of carriers for when he gets too tired on a hike, and multiple outfits for any weather or occasion. Because of him, I have made new friends and discovered restaurants that I would never have known about had I not searched for dog–friendly businesses. Stitch has even accompanied me at the table, with his stroller in place of a chair as if he were just another human. For those of you who also look at your dog with a deep connection fostered by loyalty and care, I hope that this book will give you meaningful meals with your pup along with fond and lasting memories.

It is my wish that you and your dog feel a bit spoiled by these recipes. The world can be hard enough as it is, and a shared meal with your steadfast companion can inject joy into any day. I hope your tail wags and your mouth begins to salivate. I hope you go to the kitchen, look down at your dog and decide that this moment calls for something a little extra special.

I would also like to thank you for getting this book, even if it was gifted to you. This book symbolizes a liking for food and a caring for your dog, and in that way, without knowing you, I already like you. I worked very hard to make sure this book contains a range of interesting yet familiar takes on my favorite things to eat, and I hope you walk away with some new go to dishes or at the very least, dog–friendly cuisine.

I look forward to hearing your feedback and continuing on my food journey with you. You can visit my official website www.TheGoddardKitchen.com for more information on what is coming up next.

Thank you again for your time and for giving your dog a loving home,

Lisa Goddard

INGREDIENTS INDEX

CONVERSION CHART

Measurement

CUP	OUNCES	MILLILITERS	TABLESPOONS
8 cup	64 oz	1895 ml	128
6 cup	48 oz	1420 ml	96
5 cup	40 oz	1180 ml	80
4 cup	32 oz	950 ml	64
2 cup	16 oz	480 ml	32
1 cup	8 oz	240 ml	16
3/4 cup	6 oz	177 ml	12
2/3 cup	5 oz	158 ml	11
1/2 cup	4 oz	118 ml	8
3/8 cup	3 oz	90 ml	6
1/3 cup	2.5 oz	79 ml	5
1/4 cup	2 oz	59 ml	4
1/8 cup	1 oz	30 ml	2
1/16 cup	1/2 oz	15 ml	1

Temperature

FAHRENHEIT	CELSIUS
100 °F	37 °C
150 °F	65 °C
200 °F	93 °C
250 °F	121 °C
300 °F	150 °C
325 °F	160 °C
350 °F	180 °C
375 °F	190 °C
400 °F	200 °C
425 °F	220 °C
450 °F	230 °C
500 °F	260 °C
525 °F	274 °C
550 °F	288 °C

Weight

IMPERIAL	METRIC
1/2 oz	15 g
1 oz	29 g
2 oz	57 g
3 oz	85 g
4 oz	113 g
5 oz	141 g
6 oz	170 g
8 oz	227 g
10 oz	283 g
12 oz	340 g
13 oz	369 g
14 oz	397 g
15 oz	425 g
1 lb	453 g

Thank you to my human and animal friends, especially Stitch and Derrick Denicola, without whom this book would not have been possible.

Additional thanks to Shelley Hennig, Rasmus Blaesbjerg, Devin Denicola, Bailey Fallon, Ruthie Holmes, Garrett Kirby, Chelsea Marcantel, Jordan Wang, AJ, Beans, Boudin, Darius, Koda, and Leslie Knope

Lisa Goddard spent her childhood in the New York tri-state area, raised by her Korean mother and Army veteran father. After earning a bachelor's degree from the University of California at Berkeley, she settled in Los Angeles where her love of animals led her to adopt a 10-week-old puppy who is now a 15-year-old senior dog. Food has been a lifelong passion of hers, so in addition to cooking for friends and family, as well as a stint as a personal chef, Lisa has also cooked for her own dog on-and-off throughout his life to ease his inflamed bowel disease. She regularly writes about food for her website TheGoddardKitchen.com, Yelp, and Hype Experiences. Lisa and her dog can usually be found either in the kitchen or exploring the food culture and dining scenes of southern California and beyond.

WE PUT THE LIT IN LITERARY

CLASHBOOKS.COM

FOLLOW US

TWITTER

IG

FB

@clashbooks